The Mysterious Book of
Old Man Poems

by Bill Gainer

The Mysterious Book of Old Man Poems
copyright © 2017 by Bill Gainer
first printing

All rights reserved.
No part of this book may be reproduced
in any manner whatsoever without written
permission except in the case of brief quotations
embodied in critical essays and articles.

Acknowledgements –
Various forms of some of these poems
have previously appeared in:

A Kiss in Hell – Tree Killer Ink, Bay Area Generations 16,
Blotterature, Convergence, Bold Monkey, Full of Crow,
Guerilla Pamphlets, In Between Hangovers,
Kissing Shadows – Tree Killer Ink, Lummox 3, Lummox 4,
Lummox 6, Louisiana Calling – NightBallet Press,
Medusa's Kitchen, Midnight Lane Boutique, Poet Hound,
Poetry Now, Poetrybay, Poems-for-All, Poor Yorick's Almanac,
Queen Ann's Revenge, Red Fez, Rusty Truck, Specious Species,
Six Ft. Swells Press, The Cutting Room Floor, The Machine,
The Naked Bulb Anthology 2016, The Trailer Park Quarterly,
This is Poetry, Tule Review, and WTF

Special appreciation to:
Evan Myquest, Sandy Thomas, and Todd Cirillo

Front cover photo by:
Sarolta Bán,
www.saroltaban.com

ISBN: 978-0-9984580-5-2
Library of Congress Control Number: 2017914184

P.O. Box 5304
San Pedro, CA 90733
www.lummoxpress.com

Printed in the United State of America

for José Montoya –

While visiting
D Street,
he pointed to my beard – said,

*You're turning chrome man,
becoming an elder.
Don't worry
you'll be alright.*

Contents –

A Round of Hash Browns	1
A Fellow Traveler	2
Saving the World from Monsters	5
It's Late and I've been Drinking	6
Women I've Loved	7
Alice	8
Another Global Warming Talking Point	9
Texas Fireflies	10
A Different Kind of Love Poem	11
The Weight of the Moon	12
1949 Till Now	14
My Boy Scout Days	15
Memories Mailed from Long Ago	16
Lonely Light	18
When the Dreams Take Me	19
You'll have to ask, *Why, why did they*	20
Death is a Lonely Business	21
The Sanctuaries	22
Shopping for a Dream	23
A Night Weeping – San Francisco	24
Hushed in Loneliness	25
A Love Poem	26
Another Summer We Weep – 2016	27
NOLA – Sings for Me	28
Fuck Hope	31
Around the End of September	32
Chairs To Go	33
Ruby S. – the reincarnation of	34
An Evening in Kansas	35
Christmas Eve with Her	36

The Mysterious Friends of Children	37
The Vocabulary of Movement	38
Going through Lists	39
A Simple Note	40
The Kings of the Hummingbirds	41
The Disappearance of Time	42
The Sad Eyed Girl	43
Blame it on the Gardenias	44
A Lonely Love	45
A Quiet Night	46
A Birthday in San Antonio	47
The Reason for the Apology	48
Frank's Bicycle	49
The "WPA" Garden Work	50
A Night Wish	51
The Late Hours	52
The Last Light of Summer	53
In the Time of Wind	54
The Great Mysteries of Nothing	55
Wearing the Clown Nose	56
Smiling like a Kid	57
A Last Drink of Water	58
The Digging	59
Wagner	60
The Quiet of it All	61
Surrendering the Leaves	62
The Joy of Crows	63
One Wish	64
The Screams of the Oleanders	65
"A Better Place to Be"	66

A Bum in Reno	67
Max Schwartz's Obituary	68
The Girl with the Pink Sock	69
The Someday Plan	70
Something Got Past the Quality Control People	72
The Reason I don't have a Unicycle	73
A Place in the Quiet	74
An Afternoon Nap	75
A Coffee Shop on San Pedro	76
The Sound of Snow	77
Kissing Shadows	78
The Hands of Winter Reaching	79
Old Burns	80
A Rickety Hotel – a Cliffside, Hwy 1, Long Ago	82
Hello Yesterday	84
Unrealized Perfection	86
The Gates of a Lifetime	87
The Music	88
Notes to a Dead Lover	89
Picking Up Beer Cans	90
The Tree Trimmers	91
A Magical Thing	92
The Absence of Charm	93
Burning Man Decompression GV, CA	94
Mr. and Mrs. Magoo take a Vacation	95
About the Cat	96
Enough to End On	97
The Wrong Side of Dirt	98
An Evening's Intrusion	101

The Mysterious Book of
Old Man Poems

A Round of Hash Browns

What do you do
when it's late
and lonely
brushes your cheek?
Listen to Tom Waits
think of all the women
you've loved –
you love.
Hope one of them
loves you back.
But hey
who knows.
Sometimes
it's just about
how much
money you got
how many drinks
you can buy
and maybe a round
of hash browns
a cup of coffee
after.
Who knows?
Who cares?
You need
somebody
to talk to
and tonight
she does too.
You both do.
Anything else
is just a morning
with a stranger
everybody
trying to make
a clean getaway.

A Fellow Traveler

Mike.
Call me Mike.
So I did.
Called him Mike.
Bought him coffee
pretty close
to ten years' worth.
We never talked
much
but sometimes.

Said he drove a cab
up in Sparks
followed a woman
down here
she left
he stayed
got a room
over at the Everhart.

There were good days
man
back when
now
not so much.

Spent most of his time
walking
nobody special
another face
on the corner
one of us –
making the rounds
finding a bench
sipping his coffee
a cigarette, maybe two

having a taste
a little something
to knock the edge off
talking to the girls
when they'd listen
waiting for the moon
to chase him home
alone
empty days.

I saw his hand go out
reach for the wall
miss.
The sidewalk
never forgives.

The young ones
walk-by
grin.
Women turned their heads
try not to look.
The little ones want to stare.
Moms pull on shirt sleeves.
I helped him up.

I haven't been drinking man
been laying off
at least
not that much.

The cancer's got me.
Three months.
They gave me three months man.
I'm down eighty pounds
the skin's turning dark.
Can't see the sparkles anymore

man.
You know how you can see
the sparkles
I can't see the sparkles
anymore man.
Can you help me
to the room?
Sixty-eight
I'm six-eighty man.
That's a good run.

I thought no
no man
it's never enough.
I lied
said, *Yeah.*

It'll be another month
a couple of days at the Hospice
somebody asking
about his daughter
nobody looking too hard
his goods in a box
out at the curb
free.

And that sign
there's always that sign
taped in the hotel window
a lonesome goodbye
to a fellow traveler
the last eulogy
of another dead soldier.

Room for rent.

Saving the World from Monsters

In science class
the thing in the jar
was still moving.
My plan was to stab it
before it got away.

They confiscated my knife
had a conference
with my mom
gave me three days detention.

Later my mom called me
a sinister little bastard
wanted to know why
I couldn't be like the other kids
and commented
They
never get caught.

It's Late and I've been Drinking

I'm sitting here
messing around
minding my own
business.
Out of the corner of my eye
I see the cat.
Then I hear the dog
bark.
Well, not really a bark
something more like burr
maybe kind of like a barff
short and low
quiet like
more just to get
my attention
than anything.
The truth is
we don't have a cat.
It's late
and I've been drinking.
Regardless
I'm glad the dog
saw it too.

Women I've Loved

Sometimes
you have to wonder
if Marilyn
ever got to
just sit by the
pool
alone
swimsuit
loose, comfortable
straps undone
hanging
hair messed
not caring
what she looked like
smoking a cigarette
sipping gin
no Kennedys
no Sinatra
no Rat Pack
just sweet dreams
of DiMaggio
red roses
and some kid
from Santa Cruz
me
sending her
love letters.

Alice

I have a feeling
I'll be buried
by strangers.
The kids grown
lost to their own lives.
Friends
a few.
Most hoping
I won't take too long.
The dog
might miss me
the cat
not so much.
We never were
that close.
So the dog it is.
If there's anything
left
it's for Alice
the dog.
Keep her happy
warm
and fed.
Don't let
the postman
try to pet her
he never was
a favorite.
And make sure
she doesn't
sleep alone.
Neither of us
ever liked
sleeping alone.

Another Global Warming Talking Point

Nipples
hard.

Even
in this heat
she still turns
heads.

Texas Fireflies

You saw them?
I'm jealous.
Did you let out a gentle
sigh
lean in
to someone
a little closer?
Set your iced tea down
leave a cool evening kiss
on a warm cheek?
Fireflies
do that
to people –
at least
they should.

A Different Kind of Love Poem

The world is full of them
the fools.
I've been there myself
sometimes wishing I wasn't
sometimes wishing I was
and sometimes
just not knowing the difference.
They're there.
Some waiting to push the button
just to hear the boom
and some waiting
to dust off their champion
after the loss
just because
they need
someone to love.

That's what I'm doing
trying to write a love poem
about you and me
with the shades pulled
and the doors closed
sitting in the cool
alone – together.

You in your slip
one barrette in your hair –
me in my shorts
one sock on
trying to figure a way
to steal a line
from John Prine
just so I can tell you
if you need a fool
to love you
I know one.

The Weight of the Moon

Anyone interested
in helping raise
the moon?

I'm in
but I'm old.

It would be nice
if you
could lend a hand.
I'm thinking
together
we can do this
heave it up
just past
the tree tops.
That'll do.

If not
I'll do what I can
stay up late
have a coffee
think about all
the other old guys
who had this job.

Wonder
how many nights
they lost
sleep

and how many nights
they just said
fuck it
and went to bed
early?

Let me know
I can use
the help.

The damn thing's
heavier
than it looks.

1949 Till Now

The year I was born
the rubble of war
lingering
the great machines
being tore down
repurposed
sold for scrap
their DNA still pulsing
in the automobiles
trucks, tanks
bombs
the spoon
that dips
my evening soup.

My Boy Scout Days

I remember those days
too many rules.
You weren't supposed to
use a firearm
unless accompanied
by an adult.
Could lead
to some very awkward
situations.

I was trying to make it through
the fire-starting class
get a merit badge
hang it on my sash
act like I was – somebody
but the troop leader
was of the opinion
that the three of us
me, and two of my brothers
enjoyed the quest for combustibility
a bit too much.
We didn't even get to keep
the water proof matches.

These days
my camping experiences
are pretty much confined
to the Travelodge, a rented car
and the waitress pouring
the morning coffee.

I'll probably go to my grave
never having started
a fire
with two sticks and a string.
Christ, the emptiness of it all.

Memories Mailed from Long Ago

The bondsman
wanted me
to put the house up
to get him out.

Later we talked.
One of us
was going kill
one of us.
We all knew it.

Three young cats,
spinning the wheel
of destiny
never worrying about
whose name
it fell on.

You can't live that wild
that long
without something
or someone
dying.

Later
after the smoke settled
and the ugliness
quieted
he moved to Mexico –

didn't last long
got sick
and died.

Me, to the mountains
to hide out.
It's been a while.

Got a card
from his third wife – Rita.
Said, *He was always glad
it wasn't you killing him.
He said, You never deserved it.*

*Be blessed
he always
loved you.*

Lonely Light

In his room
alone
he bleeds light
not enough to bother
the neighbors
but enough
to attract the moths
for the cat
to play with.
Enough
to keep him up
late
write poems by.
Enough
to make him wish
he wasn't so
goddamned lonely.

When the Dreams Take Me

I think of you
smiling in the dark
beside me.

You'll have to ask,
Why, why did they

Yeah
there was another woman
Patzie.
They wrote love poems
to one another.
Some true, some not
they had fun.
She got sick, took a while
gone now.
She was a little older
him – banged around some.
It showed.
Time
gave them about
that much
not much
about as much
as you can squeeze
between two fingers
when pinched
tight –
not much.
Yeah
they used to write
love poems
to one another.
He
still does.

Death is a Lonely Business
                      for Lara

Should go
but I'm not
to the service.

Wonder
what she'd
look like
in green?

They won't miss me.
If they do
I'll just tell them
I was home
alone
with my thoughts.

We never had
a lot to say.
Just friends
in passing
mostly
hi, bye
how you been
missed you.

The rest
I'll keep
to myself.

I think
she would have
looked
lovely
in green.

We'll never know.

The Sanctuaries

Used to work the factories
mostly the graveyard shift
a lot of years ago.
No demons, vampires
monsters, or ghosts
just tired souls and the job.
In the morning
the sanctuaries –
Bob's Place, the Busy Bee Club
The Steamroller, Pete's Hideout
the Chittenden Pass Inn, Whiskey Hill.
In those days
a long list of honky tonks
and dive bars
a gang of bartenders
who knew how to
keep secrets
He comes, he goes
no – ain't seen him – not today.
A jukebox
always hungry.
The same tired gal
needing a last dance
before heading home
from the packing plant.
It's always too early, too late
never the right time.
You order another round –
a short beer – a straight shot.
The rumble of the machines
still grinding in your ears.
The blink of the neon –
the night's
life support.
You hope no one
starts a fight.

Shopping for a Dream

Maybe they have
something else
something
that will take me places –
places
where the women
glide
pull their faces
close
outline your lips
with whiskey dipped
fingertips
offer one last
kiss
before never
saying
goodbye.

A Night Weeping – San Francisco

At the window table
street side
the Asian girl's tongue
pink
smooths her lipstick
waits.

Her companion
sips his tea
misses it.

Love's – want – wish
kissed into a napkin.
The busboy
cleans the table
dreams left
on the smudged edge
of a half full
wine glass
the dishwasher
doesn't care.
The waiter –
tip
never enough.

The Asian girl –
smile broken
follows him past
the register
out the door.

The chill
of a night weeping
holds her tighter
than he
ever will.

Hushed in Loneliness

Some go years
without the feeling
then it comes
one day, every day
relentless
one word
from one person
driving you back to the child
who spent the long hours
alone
watching the cold
through a cracked single pane
window
knowing – all time does
is push
all you want
farther away.

The ones like me
have learned to hold back
knowing each day
each push
makes the reaching
for the pistol
that much easier
but we don't.

Others are able to let go
become hushed in their loneliness.
Others
get lost in empty dreams
wander beyond rescue
melt in hurt
until time
calls
no more.

A Love Poem

I hate
how I miss you.

Another Summer We Weep – 2016

It's been ugly for a while.
Way past time
to weep.
Way past time
to stop.

NOLA – Sings to me
for Maddie Levy

Sing to me
point a finger
sip a cold drink
and smile.

Christ
somedays
the gods are good
even to old men.
Somedays.

So
somebody told you
I like Tom Waits.
Yeah, we hung out
some
him on the radio
me in the corner
booth
drank a little bourbon
smoked a few
cigarettes
talked
quiet like.
You know how you do
when you're drinking
bourbon
talk – quiet like.

I think
you were mentioned –
you didn't have a name
then
you were just somebody
I needed to know.

Maybe you and I
can do that sometime.
You can sing to me
the way you do
soft like.
I'll listen.
That's what I'll do
listen.
Maybe you can
lean in
my way –
just a little?
I like that.
Close.
You know.

So, thanks for dropping by
sharing the tune
waving.
I'll sleep good tonight
kid
dream big
all about you.

Did they tell you
I fall in love –
a lot.
Can't help it
it's another thing I do
fall in love –
a lot.

A soft voice
a teasing smile
a finger bent

just right –
Christ – I'm hooked.

That's why I keep
a list –
the women I'll love
forever.
You're on it.
Number 974.

Sleep good kid.
Thanks for the song.
You sing it better
than Tom
ever did.

Fuck Hope

How long
can you believe
in an empty faith
before saying
fuck hope
pulling the pistol
telling the clerk
to hand it over
wishing
for a clean
getaway.

Yeah –
go with wishes.
They're easier
to accept
for the longshots
they are –
seldom break
hearts
and there's always
the chance
of coming up big.

Hope
fuck hope.
There are too many strings.
You have to believe
in things
the mysteries of god
why leaves are always
orphans
and that the death of Jesus
wasn't
a suicide.

Around the End of September

A different kind
of warm
settles in.
Not too hot
the sticky gone.
It's nice.
I like it
we can sleep
close.

Chairs To Go

Saw a guy
walking downtown
carrying a chair
a kitchen chair
he was carrying it
like a surfboard
except with legs
you know.
I imagine
he's ordering them
the chairs
one at a time
to go.

Ruby S. – the reincarnation of

Saw your picture
in the obits.
Christ, you were beautiful.
I could have loved you
but we missed
each other
time
place
circumstance.
It all runs together.
Maybe next time?
I'll keep an eye open
ask around
now
that I know
what you look like.

An Evening in Kansas

The tornado
fifteen minutes
in the storm shelter.
Climbing out
she falls to her knees
screams, *Thank you*
to a vengeful god
the kids
cling
scared.
The old man
surveys the damage
in a low breath
mumbles
Christ
I just mowed
the lawn.
None of it
makes sense
not even
the quiet.

Christmas Eve with Her

No cooking prep
no mistletoe hanging
no rum drinks to set a mood.
Just the continuing drone
of knives being sharpened
coming from the kitchen.
Lots of knives.

The Mysterious Friends of Children

It's okay
you don't have to believe
in them
the mysterious friends
of children.
They don't care.

It's easier if you do though
because they're with us
me, you, everybody –
us, all of us.

They're all around
with their tricks
their magic
letting things happen.
It's what they do –
let things happen.

If you haven't
seen them
don't look so hard
they'll find you
perhaps
they already have
it's hard to tell
when they do.

If the milk should spill
or a glass should break
it's a good sign
they're here
the mysterious friends
of children.
Watching – watching over
us all.

The Vocabulary of Movement

Modern dance
an acquired taste.
At the end
of the performance
all I could think
was
those girls
really need
to wash
their feet.

Going through Lists

They send email
reminders
of people's birthdays.
When I go through the list
all that comes to mind is
Christ, you're still alive.

A Simple Note

Her picture
pulls the old man's
breath
slow
lets him stare
without notice
think about things
she might know
too.

His glance
away
makes sure
he's alone.
His thoughts
deep.

He writes
a simple note
I only wish
time
was kinder.

Drops it
in the mail
no address
to or from
no stamp.

The Kings of the Hummingbirds

When does it become
easy to decide
if their breath
matters –
the ones with fur
scales
feathers
the winged things
bugs
rocks
dirt
water
mud?

Maybe we should leave
the decisions
to the Kings
of the Hummingbirds.

Let them decide
if the roses
gardenias
the wind
should stay.

Let them decide
who
should fill
the feeders.

The Disappearance of Time

The weeds in the planter
yellow.
The leaves blown
into hiding.
Summer never said
goodbye
just moved off
a little at a time
and gone.

The Sad Eyed Girl

She quit shaving
her eyebrows
looks like Frida
now
except
with short hair
and boy's shoes.
She's convinced
nobody loves her –
him, her
nobody.
You want to ask
if anyone's
touched it
yet
but you don't.
Still
for her sake
you hope
someone has.

Blame it on the Gardenias

She asked
what smelled
so nice?
I said
I thought it was
you.

She pulled close
said
Whatever happens
from here
we'll blame it on
the gardenias.

I bought drinks
we danced
whispered
she left the flower
in her hair.

We woke in the morning
knowing
the trouble
had just begun
and
loved it.

Even now
all these years
later
we still
blame it on
the gardenias.

A Lonely Love

One room
a kitchenette
and a bath.
Six-fifty a month
her secret place
where she keeps
the little things
the memories –
one chess piece
a little silver happy-face
drawn on its side –
a pill bottle
three lipstick
stained
cigarette butts
inside
the lid tight –
a pillow to hold
when she's lonely
it smells like
someone else –
and the corner of the bed
where she sits
rocks herself
and wishes
just wishes.

A Quiet Night

Sipping
whiskey
the pistol
resting
the knife
folded
coffee
cold
papers
scattered
all pretending
it's a party
of lost invitations.
It's quiet
nothing asks
to be done
you could turn
the light on
but why?

A Birthday in San Antonio

Yeah, it's been a while.
Still missing you –
lots.
That won't stop
no matter how many
birthdays go by.

You still wear that
red lipstick?
It's your color.
I can see you
blowing out the candles
now.

Make a wish kid
something big.
I got mine
you're in it.
Happy Birthday
to you.

The Reason for the Apology

I just wanted you
to shut the fuck
up.
Not go away
and die
or anything.
Just
shut the fuck
up.

Frank's Bicycle

They came and took Frank away.
Packed up all his things
him and the cat
and took him away.
Everything but Frank's bicycle.
I could see it from the bathroom window
leaning against the side of the garage.
He used to ride it around the neighborhood.
Looked like Kermit the Frog in that
Muppet movie.
He waved, talked to the folks
cruised around
and waved some more.
He was 88, a retired carpenter
made things, wonderful things.
He made an alarm for his fishing poles
wired it to his boat to warn when something
was biting.
Used an old beer can, a flash light battery
a couple of small light bulbs
and an old doorbell ringer.
He said the trick was to wire the lights in series
and the ringer in parallel.
That way when fishing at night
he could tell which pole was hitting
and only needed one doorbell.
He gave me one for Christmas once.
It's around someplace.
His boy put the house up for sale
said he was tired of taking care of it.
I'd ask about Frank.
The kid just said, *He ain't coming back, man.*
A while ago I noticed Frank's bicycle was gone.
I guess it got tired
of waiting, too.

The "WPA" Garden Work

Left the window open last night
the crickets were talking
hadn't heard them in a while.
They acted like they knew me.
I said, *Hey-man*, asked how long
they'd be working.
One of them answered
We're pulling a Graveyard
tonight man.
I thought about closing the window
but didn't want to be rude.
One of them asked, *Why?*
I said, *Nothing man, nothing.*
It was quiet for a minute
then everybody went back to work.
I slept on the couch
they were gone this morning.
Tonight,
it was just the clean up crew.

A Night Wish

A few photos
remain
other than that
she's mostly gone.
Time shuffles
memory.

You sit
wait
wish
maybe tonight
she'll return
maybe not
but maybe

if only
in a dream?

The Late Hours
for D.R.

Read your poems this morning
once again, they brought the magic
left me smiling.
I imagine
in the late hours
your rooms fill
with mysterious visitors
and odd creatures
on wondrous
adventures.
I am always thankful
they enjoy your company
leave you
with a bit of something
to talk about.

The Last Light of Summer

The weather
finally starting to turn
but with the fires and all
the sun still casts
its orange shadows.
Gives an old man
uneasy feelings.
Been through it before.
The trees in the back
still show their scars.
Mine
they're a bit harder to read
especially this time of year
with my heavy coat
and dark pants.
Grief likes to keep its
secrets warm.
Like most old men
I hide mine.

In the Time of Wind

Pushing the leaves
to the ground
trading beauty
for safety
a quilt
of disarray
hiding the world
from
its flaws.
Making us all
wish
winter
had a different
friend.

The Great Mysteries of Nothing

We fixed up the back some
so we could sit out there
and look at nothing.
It was lovely.

Then the deer came
and ate all
of the nothing.
Now
when we're sitting out there
looking at nothing
we have nothing
to look at.

I spoke
with a few friends
the outdoorsy type.
They all agreed
there is nothing
we can do.

So, we're back
to looking
at the pre-nothing
nothing
before we had nothing
to look at.

I put a light
out there –
switched
and everything.
It looks lonely
with nothing
but nothing
to shine on.

Wearing the Clown Nose

If you want to be taken seriously
you have to get their attention
first.
Once you do
then bring in
the monkeys.

Smiling like a Kid

Sometimes
when it's late –
the bourbon's warm
and no one's
looking
I pee over the edge
of the porch.
Pretending to shoot down
Nazis.
I swear
if you look real hard
you can see the wreckage
of a Messerschmitt
in the roses.

A Last Drink of Water

There's an old woman
upstairs sleeping
without me.

The problems
of the world
are someone else's
worry
at least for tonight.

I'm tired.

All I've got left is –
I love you
and I do.

Christ
it's quiet.
I hope I don't
wake her.

The Digging

I've taken up
a new pastime
digging
in the back.
Moving this pile
to that pile
and that pile
to the other pile.
Sometimes
I make a new pile.
Most days Kae St. Marie
comes out
says
*I have a cold drink
for you.
You might want to
come in
before it gets too hot.*
Some days I do
some days I don't
depends
on the digging.
She says
people ask about me.
She tells them
*It keeps him home
off the bourbon
and he seems
to enjoy it
the digging.*

Wagner

He introduces me
to rainbows.
He's good at it
I've met quite a few
because of him.
He knows their names.
Yes,
rainbows have names.

He's got a good eye
points things out –
the fairies
their magic –
how the light turns
in the evening –
the fog melts
with the morning –
and how the night
creatures
bring gifts
if you just leave
a window
unlatched.

Yeah – he sees things.
Little things.
Things you don't
always notice
when busy
pushing
through time.

The Quiet of it All

Looking
out the kitchen window
I mentioned
I just raked the leaves
Rose (the dog) is out there
making a mess.

Kae St. Marie
stirring the soup
answered with
*Now you know
how I felt
when the kids
fucked-up
the snow.*

She'd told me before
how she liked to sit
with her coffee
look out
at the snow
and just listen
to the quiet of it all.

It seems so much
darker
when told today –
*the kids
fucked-up
the snow.*

I thought it best
to just compliment
the soup
*good,
very good.*

Surrendering the Leaves

Winter's visit
demands
the surrendering
of the leaves.

The old men
in their heavy coats
and the old women
in their hats
hold tight
to what was –

the bare branches
of hope, wish
and dream –

to be held
loved
and never said
goodbye to.

The Joy of Crows
for Lew Welch

Having never found
the comfortable place
where love is simple
and the others just let it be.

No
they have rules
fucking rules
always
the fucking rules.

Always an expectation
not to be lived up to.
Always broken things
kept in secret places
inside
where
yesterday's dreams
scrape tired wishes
from hearts too worn
to heal.

Yes the revolver
is kept close
waiting for its note.
Something short:

Cremation –
somewhere out of the way
where the bastards
can't complain
about the smoke
and the crows can roll
in my ashes
with joy.

One Wish

I wish
dogs could talk.
Cats, not so much.
They already have
a thousand ways
of telling the world
to fuck-off.
No need for another.

The Screams of the Oleanders

The Oleanders
have once again
been butchered.
Their skeletal remains
a tribute to my mastery
of residential yard care.

"A Better Place to Be"

It's not the muscle
or tendon
that keep the bones
from collapsing.
It's the rust, stale grease
and corner scum
of the factory floors
holding them up.

Too many years
on the assembly line
pulling the future – from the past.
Too many dreams built
for no one to sleep with –
but there's always
that one last cigarette
a cool place out of the sun
and someone
to pour the whiskey.

We grow old
and time wars on.
We've built our empires –
the young ones
are building theirs.

These days – it's different
the factories – gone.
All that's pulled
from the past
rusts.

It's a new world,
some say
A better place
to be.

A Bum in Reno

With a voice
gentle
he asked if I had a dollar.
I gave him two.

Then about the dime
pointed
said, *You dropped it.*
I said, *Yeah.*

Thanks
not much of a word.
He said it twice
his eyes
once more.

I told him
Be safe man.

He said
It's hard.

Max Schwartz's Obituary

I haven't seen it in a while –
Max's obituary.
He was a dear friend –
goofy in his ways
always asking me
to talk to this or that
newspaper person for him.
After he moved back
to Woodstock
I'd get these late night calls
we'd talk –
catch up on whatever needed
catching up on.
He would always hit me
for a little something.
I still laugh
he called all the way
across the country
to borrow five bucks.
I'd put a little extra
in the envelope –
try to make sure
he had enough for his tea
and to throw a little –
a stranger's way.
He was always generous
like that –
one of the *Mad Poets
of San Francisco.*
He knew little of wealth
but in him
carried a fortune.
I miss those calls
addressing those envelopes
and Max.
I miss Max.

The Girl with the Pink Sock

She carries
her cell phone
in a pink
sock.
Says it's her
weapon
of choice.
Learned it watching
old
prison movies.
Says it's better
than a bar
of soap
and the *Screws*
if they notice
just think it's
cute.

The Someday Plan

I want my ashes
in a cocktail
shaker
silver plated
knocked around a little
vintage.
Just so the lid
stays on.

At the funeral
play the Stone's
"Sympathy for the Devil"
and maybe Solomon Burke's
"Can't Nobody Love You"
just so Kae St.Marie knows
I do ...
Otis's - "I've Been Loving You
Too Long"
Because you gotta have
Otis.
Close it out
with The Isley Brothers
"Shout."
Join in
raise your arms up, shout – loud.
I like a noisy crowd.

A dear friend
out of New Orleans
says he'll hoist my final
toast
something legendary
make the old men
sit quiet, reflect

the ladies sip their bourbon
ask for another – smile, blush
and the lovers pull close
not caring who sees.

I'm hoping
he doesn't miss
the show.
There have been
a couple of
nasty incidents.
He likes to chase
crazy women.
Most of them
carry knives.

When it comes around
you're invited.
Stop by
have a cold drink.
It could be a potluck
would be nice
if you brought
a little something.

Something Got Past
the Quality Control People

There was something floating
in the Top Ramen.
Not sure what it was –
a sample
a mistake
a test marketing ploy
a piece of a finger?
Regardless
I ate it.

The Reason I don't have a Unicycle

If I did
I'd want
to ride it.
Could be
dangerous.
Lean back
close your eyes
let your imagination
get away with you.
See what I mean?
That's why
I don't have
a unicycle.

A Place in the Quiet

The hour
when that one last
exhale
changes it all.

Nothing before
if it ever did
matters.

The light's angle
thins –
the day's eyes
close – slow.

You're left
to yourself
finally.

An Afternoon Nap

The flight didn't really last that long
but there was that moment
that one moment when it felt like the sky
had no bottom.
Looking down
blue, gray, a mist of pink
there was nothing to see –
no birds, dust, leaves blowing
just me, for a moment free
from whatever it is
chains us
to ourselves.

A Coffee Shop on San Pedro

Iced tea
and yoga pants.
One gets me
in the door
the other
keeps me there.

And oh yeah –
the company
of strangers.

But
if you want to
place a bet –
go with
the yoga pants.

The Sound of Snow

It's hard to hear
the snow.
Sometimes
you think maybe
but no.

The wind's tongue lashing
trees cracking
tires splashing
but the snow
no.

It's mostly
a gentle whisper
a cold kiss
something
to wipe from
an eyelash
a smile from a lover
a friend.

Never a long
goodbye
a voice
raised
or a hint
of tricks
to be played.

Only the chilled
breath of quiet
and the settling
of the snow
as it welcomes
winter.

Kissing Shadows
for A.M., 3/30/1936 - 7/9/2016

Under the hum
of a tired Sacramento
air-conditioner
we said goodbye.
I kissed her shadow
she kissed mine.
We both knew
whatever time does
however dark
it gets
we may never again
but our shadows
always will
find
one another.

The Hands of Winter Reaching

It's nights like these that bother me
the cool breeze of fall has arrived
not threatening, but warning.
The threat comes later
along with the promise.
Know winter smiles
with one tooth missing
but bites just as hard.
And tonight's breeze
just a warning
winter is coming
for you.

Old Burns

I knew a guy
back in the 60s
had a scar
from a clothes iron
on his belly
just above
his belt line.

You could tell
it was an iron
kind of looked like
a just launched
spaceship.
It must have hurt like
hell.

He said it happened
in the Navy
loading shells
over by Vietnam.

He lied
let the truth slip
one night –
too many cocktails
at the Busy-Bee Club.

His second wife
had put it to him –
she liked to fight
dirty.

Cost him fifteen hundred
dollars
to replace three of her teeth
from the punch
that knocked her out
that night.

In those days
they called it passion.
When the blood boiled
you let it
boil.

He said the marriage lasted
another year
until she came at him
with the pruning shears
and even though
she'd moved to Reno
he still carried
a Mexican switchblade.
Just in case
she still loved him.

A Rickety Hotel –
a Cliffside, Hwy 1, Long Ago

I think I
rented a room there
once.
Was asked to leave
because of the dancing.
My partner was a big girl
thick thighs,
we liked to Mambo.
I thought it was my moves
causing the world to sway.
They said it was the foundation
slipping.
She called me
her
Delicious
Little Peach.
We've lost touch
but I still remember those
thick thighs
and every now and then
in a crowded room
a quiet bar
or a sleepy bus stop
I'll bust a move –
Just in case
she's out there
looking for me.
Christ, I'm sure
she don't look
the same either
but it would be nice
to hear her voice,

*Don't I know you,
you ever spend time
up on the coast?
I used to dance with
a guy up there.
He drank bourbon.
You drink
bourbon?
You dance?*

Hello Yesterday

That's it man
they all wanted
me to be
something else.
Didn't happen.
This is it.
The ghost
of could have been
the shadow of what was.
Me.

They don't need
to love me
you either –
but I do wish ...
maybe somebody would,
just to even it out
a little.
But hey
anyway it comes
I'm good.

I know
it's theirs –
the world.
What else can they do
to let me know.
You'd never guess
a scar
could weigh so much
but
when you've been in the fight
this long
the ugly
adds up.

The clock
ticking – man.
Time,
tick, tick ...
time
running low
red light flashing.
Time.

If you gotta
hate me –
do.
I'm okay with it.
If you're just passing –
how about a cigarette
a light,
maybe a sip of something
that gets down in there
heats it up.
We'll share
the quiet.
No need to be friends
just the faces of lonely
looking across the table
and the dark.

There it is –
time.
I could have been.
Gone now.
It's what I was
what I am.
So, hello yesterday
Thanks for waiting –
I'll see you there
soon.

Unrealized Perfection

There are
a lot ways
to do a good suicide.
Some so beautiful
so perfect –
they just slip by.
Even the note
gets over looked.

The Gates of a Lifetime

When the factories
sang for me.
I heard their song.
Now no one knows
my work.
How the hand welcomed
the wrench
became one
pulling
all that's loose
tight.
The machines
waiting to be loved
worked and love back.
In the last days
walking the floors
saying goodbye
not to the men
but to the sounds
having shared
their secrets
of the weak
being broken.
Looking back
the shadows
ask
who will you be
without me?
The truck
reluctant to start
slow
through the gates.
The guard doesn't know
I will not
be back.

The Music

She reached over
dimmed the music
said, *I couldn't hear
you breathe.*

Notes to a Dead Lover

She sends notes
into the ether
apologies to a dead
lover
sorry you missed
so much living
today was special
someone kissed me
I think
you would have liked him.

Picking Up Beer Cans

Feeling better today
still a bit fuzzy
don't want to
kill anyone
though.
Yesterday
I did.
Today
I'm good.

The Tree Trimmers

The Mexican kids
showed up
trimmed the trees
from the power lines.

They did it
gently.
The jays and sparrows
didn't seem
to notice.
Even the young oaks
didn't act scared.

Twenty minutes later
the squirrels returned
to their gossip.

Two houses down
the work continued.

A Magical Thing

She told me
always embrace
to the left.
That way
you're heart
to heart.
And if you hold
tight enough
and long enough
the beats become
one.
Said it is a magical
thing.
Asked
if I wanted to try?
Said the secret is
to never
let go.

The Absence of Charm

Since
the bookstore cat
Romeo
died
no one says
watch the door
don't let the cat
out – please.

Even though
I seldom
saw the cat
and I still don't –
I wish they would
say it.

Seems
such a charming way
to let the world know
you've come
you've gone.

Burning Man Decompression GV, CA

The bar was loud,
a bald-headed short guy
kilt freshly pressed
dancing –
like a drunken cat
chasing a dot on the floor
he had the moves.
No music.

The kid in the Army uniform
with his little
branding irons
brought his flame throwing
machine inside.
It was like
a jet plane
when he fired
the thing off.

The sound system
had its problems
Jesse, the sound man, tried
several times.
He tried.

Christ –
nobody heard nothing.

I cut my reading
in half –
thanked the crowd
and headed out.
The guy
working the door
said – *I really liked your stuff
Ed.*

Mr. and Mrs. Magoo take a Vacation

It's me and Kae St. Marie
and the odd dreams again.
I'm like Mr. Magoo
her, Mrs. Magoo.

We're at Disneyland
checking out
the restrooms
Oh, this is nice.
Look, they got soap!

We're up to 13 now
still working on it.

And the dreams
still come.
But I'm sleeping good.
Mrs. Magoo too.

About the Cat

She said
*Don't ask
about the cat.*
I said, *What cat?*
She said
*I told you
not to ask.*

Enough to End On

As long as I got
a couple of bucks
can find a warm
barstool
have the strength
to tell one
listen to one –
another lie
wander home
and dream
they were all true
the lies.
That's enough.

The Wrong Side of Dirt

Visited an old friend
Bob
was glad to see that someone
probably his sister
the one from up in Reno
finally placed
a headstone.

After wiping the snow
and reading the inscription:

James Robbins Gardiner (Bob)
an extraordinary artist
a creative thinker
March 19, 1951 – April 21, 2005

I thought, *This is it – huh?*
The guy was once somebody
had won one of the big ones
an Academy Award
way back when
for a stop-motion-animated
short film thing
he did in college.

I heard it was down hill
from there.
That his world
was an alien place
it didn't love him
as much as we did.

Talk was
he took the dark way out –
a piece of cord
a rented room
the city cops
pushing the door in
him hanging there
done.

His sister said –
because of the way
he left
the priest wouldn't
bury him
so they did
some kind of Indian thing
burnt some sage
banged some drums
and chanted something
that meant something
to somebody
who knows?

After all the crap –
the craziness
the booze
the dope
the good times
the bad
the women
the fighting

the falling in love
I always loved
the falling in love
even the meds
yeah they put you on the meds
when they think you've gone
a little goofy.

After all of it
here I am
an old man
left standing in the snow
talking to an old friend
who's long gone
wondering
which one of us
is truly
on the wrong side
of the dirt.

An Evening's Intrusion

On the porch
wishing a cigarette
the first sip
of bourbon
he looks
a bit younger
with the second
at peace.
It's his eyes.

The neighbor lady
Ruth
widowed a decade
from her porch
waves.
He waves back.

The street lights
stagger to life
hide the sky.
One by one
the stars go out.

Bill Gainer is a storyteller, humorist, poet, and a maker of mysterious things. He earned his BA from St. Mary's College, and his MPA from the University of San Francisco. He is the publisher of the PEN Award winning R. L. Crow Publications, and is the ongoing host of Red Alice's Poetry Emporium (Sacramento, CA). Gainer is internationally published, and known across the country for giving legendary fun filled performances. His work is not for sissies. Visit him in his books, at his personal appearances, or at his website: billgainer.com.

The LUMMOX Press publishes chapbooks,
the Little Red Book series, perfect bound books
(the Respect series), a poetry anthology (yearly)
and e-copies. The stated goal of the press
is to elevate the bar for poetry, while bringing
the 'word' to an international audience.
We are proud to offer this book
as a part of that effort.

For more information and to see
our growing catalog of choices, please go to
www.lummoxpress.com

Made in the USA
San Bernardino, CA
17 February 2018